The Devil and H

James Gordon Bennett, the Penny Press and the Rise of Modern Communication

Dwight L. Teeter

with
David Doyle

First Inning Press
in conjunction with the
Intercollegiate Online News Network

Tennessee Journalism Series

Table of Contents

Preface...4
  Tennessee Journalism Series...4
  ABOUT THE AUTHOR...6
  ABOUT THE DESIGNER..6

1. Introduction..7

2. Benjamin Day and the New York Sun....................... 9
  THE MOON HOAX 10

3. James Gordon Bennett and the New York Herald...........13
  BENNETT MAKES ENEMIES.. 15
  Sidebar: BENNETT UNDER SIEGE 17
  Sidebar: THE HERALD'S SENSATIONALIST REPORTING......... 17

4. Warring Papers: Horace Greeley and the New York
Tribune 18
  EXPANDING NEWS COVERAGE.................................. 20

5. Convergence, 19th Century style 22
  POPULATION GROWTH AND URBANIZATION........................ 22
  THE RACE FOR NEWS... 23
  STEAM POWER AND FASTER PRESSES 23
  A GROWING NETWORK OF RAILROADS 23
  REAL MODERNITY BEGINS: THE TELEGRAPH......................... 24
  CONVERGING WITH TODAY....................................... 26

The First Amendment 27
  Religion 28
  Speech... 30
  Press.. 32
  Assembly.. 36
  Petition.. 37
  History 39

Preface

Many of the things that happened first during the Penny Press era have become the staples of today's journalism: the dominance of non-partisan news; the emphasis on speed; new areas of reporting, including sports reporting; an expansion of readership to include working classes.

The list could go on. Much that is on that list began with James Gordon Bennett.

Bennett, a 27-year-old Scotsman with a university education in economics, arrived in the United States in 1822. He failed in repeated journalistic ventures in the U.S. before founding the New York Herald in 1835. Within six years, however, he rode the crest of the development of penny newspapers to wealth and power, becoming a leading editor of his time. Bennett didn't invent the penny press, but his success with the Herald made him a captain of the emerging newspaper industry.

This book takes up the context of the Penny Press facing Bennett in the 1830s and 1840s, considers the 21st century buzzword "media convergence" with a 19th century spin, and looks at some of Bennett's enduring innovations—and those of a despised competitor, the even-more-famous Horace Greeley, who started his New York Tribune in 1841.

In this book, you'll read about

- Benjamin Day and the Sun
- James Gordon Bennett and the Herald
- Horace Greeley and the Tribune
- The 19th century version of convergence

The book also contains a bonus chapter on the First Amendment.

This book is part of the **Tennessee Journalism Series**.

Tennessee Journalism Series

The **Tennessee Journalism Series** is a set of texts and instructional material developed by the faculty of the University of Tennessee School of Journalism and Electronic Media for journalism students and instructors around the world.

The idea behind the series is "multimedia first."

That is, these books are built for the iPad and contain a variety of multimedia elements: text, audio, video, photo galleries, interactive images, and interactive reviews and quizzes.

At present, nine books are available on iBookstore for download to the iPad:

Introduction to Journalism

Reporting: An Introduction

Photojournalism

The First Amendment

Media Reporting

Feature Writing

Going Online: How to Start a Scholastic News Website

How to Get a Job in TV (Denae D'Arcy)

Writing Like a Journalist (Jim Stovall)

Other books in active development include:

Television News (Sam Swan)

Journalism and Social Media (Ioana Coman and Margaret Grigsby)

Legal Issues for Journalism Students (Mike Martinez and Dwight Teeter)

The British Media (Mark Harmon)

Full descriptions of the books available with their iBookstore, Kindle and Amazon links can be found at http://tnjnseries.com.

ABOUT THE AUTHOR

Dwight L. Teeter Jr. is a professor of journalism and electronic media at the University of Tennessee. He joined the University of Tennessee faculty as Dean of the College of Communications in 1991 and served in that role until 2002. Teeter previously taught at six universities, including Iowa State, Wisconsin, Washington, Kentucky, Wisconsin-Milwaukee, and Texas, where he was the first holder of the William P. Hobby Centennial Professorship from 1984-1987. He has written several books, including *Law of Mass Communications* (with Bill Loving of East Carolina and previously Professor Harold L. Nelson of Wisconsin, and Professor Don. R. Le Duc, Wisconsin-Milwaukee), which is now in its 13th edition. Professor Teeter has won several awards during his career, including the Society of Professional Journalists Distinguished Teacher Award, the University of Tennessee College of Communications Distinguished Research Award, and a Distinguished Service Award from the Association for Education in Journalism and Mass Communication, an organization for which he served as president from 1985-1986.

ABOUT THE DESIGNER

David Doyle designed the iPad edition of this book and contributed much, including the nultimedia items, to its content. He is a student of Journalism and Information Sciences at the University of Tennessee. As a freelance technology and entertainment writer, his contributions to the Knoxville, TN altweekly newspaper *Metro Pulse* have earned two Golden Press Card awards from the East Tennessee Society of Professional Journalists. In 2012, Doyle was recognized for his academic and professional accomplishments by the webcomic and gaming and technology news outlet Penny Arcade through their annual scholarship, making him the first journalism student to receive this award.

1. Introduction

He looked demonic with his disconcerting glare. He was afflicted with extreme strabismus, resulting in wildly crossed eyes.

But despite his appearance, James Gordon Bennett succeeded mightily in journalism and in communication innovation. He came to be hated for his combativeness, for his journalistic sensationalism, and for his disdain for mid-19th century moral standards, but he set the pace toward modern media.

Bennett, a 27-year-old Scotsman with a university education in economics, arrived in the United States in 1822. He failed in repeated journalistic ventures in the U.S. before founding the *New York Herald* in 1835. Within six years, however, he rode the crest of the development of penny newspapers to wealth and power, becoming a leading editor of his time. Bennett didn't invent the penny press, but his success with the *Herald* made him a captain of the emerging newspaper industry.

This book takes up the context of the Penny Press facing Bennett in the 1830s and 1840s, considers the 21st century buzzword "media convergence" with a 19th century spin, and looks at some of Bennett's enduring innovations—and those of a despised competitor, the even-more-famous Horace Greeley, who started his *New York Tribune* in 1841.

James Gordon Bennett

2. Benjamin Day and the New York Sun

The penny press in the United States began with a struggling New York printer whose business was failing during the financial recession in 1833, which also was a time of a cholera epidemic in the city. The dire financial straits of Benjamin Day were the mother of a great invention: the New York Sun, a newspaper that revolutionized the publishing industry even as Day himself took on the establishment press of his era.

In a desperate effort to save his business, New York printer Benjamin Day launched a tiny four-page newspaper called the New York *Sun* in 1833, with sheets measuring just 7 5/8 by 10 1/4 inches. Sold at only a penny a copy, *The Sun* was a real departure from the six-cent price on other papers.

Many people could not afford to spend six cents on a paper, when that amount of money would buy a good dinner or a pint of whiskey. In 1833, there really was no paper for the middle or working classes of New York, just establishment papers that served a commercial elite and that generally served up stale news lifted from other publications. Day's new paper largely ignored government and politics, economics and editorial statements, leaving that fare to the six-penny establishment press.

Luckily for Day, out-of-work printer George Wisner showed up during *The Sun*'s first week of publication. For $4 a week, he began reporting on New York's police courts. Police court sessions provided brief human-interest morality tales, often making fun of the down-and-out.

Wisner's reporting was something new. Newspapers of the United States during the 1830s generally did not have reporters. Their contents were assembled by publisher/printers who clipped articles and essays from other newspapers, or who published material brought to the printing house, often writings donated by politicians or essayists trying to get their views into print.

Publisher Day's quick financial success caused him to boast about the importance of his little newspaper. Day wrote that he would conduct an independent paper:

"With TRUTH for our motto we alike disregard libel suits of the house-breaker, and the money of the office seeker. And whenever the villainous conduct of a man, or a body of men—(no matter to what they belong)—

may deserve exposure—so sure as we hold with our hands the whip so sure will we "Lash the rascals naked through the world."

The Sun did begin the change in the United States away from newspapers that had financial ties to political parties or politicians, so the idea of "independence" was rather remarkable at the time. *The Sun* began to show how large circulation, plus the rise of mass advertising, could allow newspapers to be independent.

Day's sensational newspaper's ability to make money led other printers—in Boston and Philadelphia as well as New York—to try that path to riches. In the 1830s, New York City's population was about 300,000. And even though there were a large number of newspapers published, Asa Greene established his *New York Transcript* six months after *The Sun's* first appearance. As Greene later noted:

"There are eleven 'large and regularly established daily papers' in this city, and with the exception of the *Courier and Enquirer*, and perhaps, the *Times*, not one of them employs a reporter, or takes any other pains to obtain accurate or correct information—on the other hand, there are two small daily NEWS papers (ourselves and our contemporary), and those two employ four reporters, exclusively to obtain the earliest, fullest and most complete intelligence of every local incident; and two of these latter arise at 3 in the morning, at which hour they attend the police courts . . . while others are obtaining correct information about the city."

THE MOON HOAX

Even today, *The Sun* is still notorious for the granddaddy of all newspaper hoaxes.

After George Wisner sold back his share and left the paper, Benjamin Day hired another reporter, Richard Adams Locke, for the then-substantial salary of $12 a week.

Locke, a graduate of England's Cambridge University, proposed a series of stories dealing with science. The stories claimed that the great astronomer Sir John Frederick William Herschel, who had an observatory near Cape Town, South Africa, had made remarkable discoveries.

In August 21, 1835, page two of the New York Sun carried this announcement:

"CELESTIAL DISCOVERIES: The Edinburgh Courant says—'We have

just learned from the an eminent publisher in this city that Sir John Herschel, at the Cape of Good Hope, has made some astronomical discoveries of the most wonderful description, by means of an enormous telescope of an entirely new principle.'" Four days later, claiming to be citing the Edinburgh Journal of Science, Richard Adams Locke's story in *The Sun* teased readers by describing the marvelous telescope in detail, claiming that Herschel had made great discoveries, including new planets in other solar systems and "a distinct view of objects on the moon." (The Edinburgh Journal of Science had ceased publication in the preceding year.)

With circulation of *The Sun* booming as readers awaited amazing revelations, on August 26, 1835 the newspaper published four columns purporting to be about astronomer Herschel's "celestial discoveries," including vegetation, the moon's atmosphere, herds of four-legged brown animals, and extensive forests. Later stories, embellished with fanciful illustrations, discussed moon men and women (who had wings and could fly) and amazing buildings, including the Temple of the Moon, made of gleaming sapphire.

The hoax was successful. Yale University science professors were among the multitudes taken in by the hoax. This fiction finally was exposed when reporter Locke confessed that he had invented the story. The hoax, however, boosted *Sun* circulation to over 19,000, at a time when New York City's largest competing newspaper—the *Courier and Enquirer*—had circulations around 4,500. Day, only 28 years old, had amassed a sizable fortune by the time he sold the *Sun* to his brother-in-law, Moses Y. Beach in 1837.

The moon hoax was denounced by other papers, of course, but the profitability of penny papers was irresistible to other publishers, including the multi-talented James Gordon Bennett.

3. James Gordon Bennett and the New York Herald

James Gordon Bennett was the penny press's quintessential American success story. A Scottish immigrant and former Washington correspondent for the New York newspapers, Bennett, with little more than a makeshift desk in a damp basement office, filled what he saw as a 20,000-paper deficit in the New York news market with his own voice: The New York Herald. With the Herald, Bennett soon became one of the best-known—and most hated—names in the newspaper industry.

James Gordon Bennett, a 27-year-old Scotsman with a university education in economics, arrived in the United States in 1822. By 1835, Bennett seemed a 40-year-old failure. He had been in the U.S. for 13 years, drifting from job to job and gaining valuable experience. He worked briefly for a Charleston, South Carolina, newspaper and then became associate editor of several newspapers, including the *New York Enquirer* and the *Courier and Enquirer,* and also covered several major criminal trials. He had a stint editing a presidential campaign newspaper in Philadelphia.

He was a Washington correspondent for those New York papers, writing with real editorial flair and winning attention for his lively descriptions of politics in the nation's capital and getting acquainted with some of the nation's political leaders.

But back in New York City, Bennett had little to show for all his efforts. He sought help from Horace Greeley (more about Greeley later) but Greeley turned him down. Still, Bennett managed to scrape together $500, rented a leaky basement room as an office, and made do with a table consisting of a wooden  plank sitting on two flour barrels as his desk for writing and taking advertisements. A printing firm, which also printed Asa Greene's *New York Transcript,* produced his tiny paper, which differed little in format or appearance from Benjamin Day's *Sun.* But Bennett explained the need for another New York paper, arguing that half of New York City's population—150,000 persons—looked at newspapers each day, with only 42,000 papers printed in the city, there was room for his *New York Herald* to sell another 20,000 copies or more.

Like Day before him, Bennett boldly promised to publish an independent paper which would "care nothing for any election, or any candidate from President down to Constable."

Aiming to out-compete the ten or so newspapers already published in the city, the second edition of Bennett's paper promised to be a relief to readers from "the dull business air of the of the large morning papers." The lively *Herald*, Bennett declared, would "exhilarate the breakfast table." Beyond that, Bennett promised his newspaper would do more than entertain. His vision included covering many organizations and activities: "'We shall give a correct picture of the world—in Wall Street—in the Exchange—in the Police Office—at the Theatres—in the Opera—in short wherever human nature or real life best displays its freaks and vagaries."

Clearly, Bennett was going to offer broader news coverage, brightly written, to be read by the elite used to the "sixpenny" dailies and to attract mass readership of common folk as well.

During the *Herald's* second year, its coverage of the Robinson-Jewett murder case boosted the *Herald's* circulation even more. Beautiful 23-year-old prostitute Helen Jewett (called "Ellen" in some accounts) was found beaten to death in a burning bed in one of New York's fanciest brothels. A watchman found a cape, identified as belonging to Richard P. Robinson, a handsome 19-year-old clerk. Robinson, said to be a regular customer of Helen Jewett, was arrested and charged with murder.

Bennett's lurid continuing coverage of the murder case and the trial gave the Robinson-Jewett story nationwide fame, as out-of-town papers picked up and repeated the lurid details. Initially, Bennett's reporting blamed Robinson, "the alleged perpetrator of this most horrid deed."

Bennett, however, later floated the idea that Jewett had been killed by someone other than Robinson, suggesting that police excluded the press from the investigation for that reason. Bennett actively and almost obsessively reported the case, and a visited the murder scene three times.

Historian John Stevens wrote that Bennett was the only journalist to visit the scene, adding, "In those days of one or two-man staffs, an editor seldom ventured outside the office." But during ten days of reporting the Robinson-Jewett case, the Herald's circulation rose from less than 4,000 to about 15,000. Whether guilty or innocent, Robinson was acquitted by a jury and moved to Texas.

BENNETT MAKES ENEMIES

As Bennett's *Herald* succeeded, he used his paper for harsh attacks on competing editors. His host of enemies grew.

Bennett, who was once was employed by James Watson Webb at the New York *Courier and Enquirer*, accused Webb of illegal stock market dealings. Webb responded violently to those criticisms three times during 1836, thrashing Bennett with his cane. Bennett used his paper to say that cowardly and villainous attacks would not make him afraid, and his paper's circulation continued to rise.

Bennett's knowledge of economics helped him to report and comment on Wall Street's financial doings. Journalism historian Willard G. Bleyer called Bennett's thorough and knowledgeable reports on Wall Street "a distinctive contribution to daily journalism." Bennett knew he was a great financial writer, and humility was not in his makeup. He boasted, "there was not a person in the lower part of the city that does not read the HERALD every day." The financial community of Wall Street – "every bank, every insurance company, every broker, take it in," and some banks even received a half-dozen copies every morning."

As Bennett's success grew, so did his arrogance. In mid-1836, the *Herald* carried Bennett's outlandish claims attacking his competitors in several issues of his paper:

"I mean to begin a new movement in the progress of civilization and human intellect. I know and feel I shall succeed. Nothing can prevent its [the *Herald's*] success. Get out of my way, ye driveling editors and driveling politicians —I am the voice of ONE crying in the wilderness, prepare ye the way of the Lord, and make his path straight.

"What is my reward? I am called a scoundrel—a villain—a depraved wretch—a base coward—a vile calumniator—a miserable poltroon. These anonymous assassins of character are leagued and stimulated by the worst men in society—by speculators—by pickpockets—by sixpenny editors—by miserable hypocrites—whose crimes and immoralities I have exposed, and shall continue to expose as long as the God of Heaven gives me a soul to think, and a hand to execute.

15

"My great purpose is to upset—reform—knock up—and revolutionize the impudent, blustering, corrupt, immoral Wall Street press."

When Bennett announced in the August 19, 1836 *Herald* that its price was doubling to two cents, he wrote: "I mean to avail myself of the high value the public very properly put on my labors, and I shall do so . . . . I want to be rich—I shall be rich."

Because he was despised by his competitors, the owners of New York newspapers tried to use Bennett's salacious reporting on scandals against him. The *Courier and Enquirer* and the *Journal of Commerce* published the following attacks on the *Herald*, which Bennett promptly re-published:

"At the request of individuals . . . we are compelled, for the first time, to soil our columns with an allusion to a beggarly outcast, who daily sends forth a dirty sheet in this city under the title of the *Herald*." [from the *Courier and Enquirer*]

"That little dirty penny paper the *Herald*, whose Editor, if he got his deserts, would be horsewhipped every day. . . ." [from the *Journal of Commerce*]

The Robinson-Jewett murder case coverage, with its grisly details about the death of the beauteous prostitute, also drew fire from his competitors, although it is unclear whether the contents of the *Herald* or its soaring circulation most irritated his critics. And, although Bennett later became more selective about accepting advertising, he outraged many by running notices that were really thinly disguised ads for prostitutes and abortionists.

Competing newspapers began a "Moral War" against Bennett in 1840, urging that decent people boycott the *Herald*. Advertisers were told not to use the *Herald*, and hotels were asked to exclude the paper. This attack on Bennett started in the *New York Signal*, and then two of Bennett's former employers joined in, Colonel James Watson Webb, editor of the *Courier and Enquirer*, and Major Mordecai Noah of the *Evening Star*. Other New York papers chimed in, including the *Journal of Commerce*, the *Express*, the *Star*, the *Commercial*, and the *American*. The *Philadelphia North American* and the *Boston Advertiser* both joined the chorus of blame.

Bennett was accused of blasphemy, indecency, lying, and libel. The "Moral War" was effective, cutting the *Herald's* circulation from 17,000 to 14,000 for several years. Although his newspaper went on to greater and greater financial success, both Bennett and his paper did so with a sleazy reputation.

Sidebar: *BENNETT UNDER SIEGE*

James Gordon Bennett made his fair share of enemies during his tenure at the *Herald*, some of whom were more than happy to express their discontent with the publisher —sometimes violently. As New York businessman and one-time mayor Philip Horne noted in his diary:

"There is an ill-looking, squinting man called Bennett, formerly connected with Webb in the publication of his paper, who is now the editor of the *Herald* . . . in which scandal is retailed to all who delight in it . . . . The man and Webb are now bitter enemies and it was nuts for Bennett to . . . [attack Webb in his paper] with evident marks of savage exultation. This did not suit Mr. Webb's fiery disposition so he attacked Bennett in Wall Street yesterday, beat him, and knocked him down."

Sidebar: *THE HERALD'S SENSATIONALIST REPORTING*

Bennett's *New York Herald* was bolstered by accounts from reporters and witnesses designed to trigger emotional responses in his readers, such as this description of the body of New York prostitute Helen Jewett, published in the *Herald* in 1836:

"The countenance was calm and passionless . . . . The left side where the fire had touched, was bronzed like an antique statue. For a few moments I was lost in admiration of this extraordinary sight—a beautiful female corpse—that surpassed the finest statue of antiquity. I was recalled to her bloody destiny by seeing the dreadful bloody gashes on the right temple, which must have caused her instantaneous dissolution . . . .What a melancholy sight for beauty, wit and talent, for it is said she possessed all, to come to such a fatal end!"

4. Warring Papers: Horace Greeley and the New York Tribune

As the penny press movement rose in popularity, so did more publishers rise to meet the public's growing demand for news. With the expansion of the news market, competing papers claimed to give bigger, better, and more bombastic offerings than their counterparts— and just as often turned on one another, putting each other in the crosshairs just as readily as they did any other target.

Mid-19th century America, buffeted by enormous problems involving slavery, sectional tensions, and swelling tides of immigration also saw an amazing new institution: a truly modern mass medium in the form of major newspapers. Archetypes of this new modernity: James Gordon Bennett's *New York Herald* and Horace Greeley's *New York Tribune*.

Greeley founded his newspaper in April, 1841, six years later than Bennett, but in two months he was asserting that the *Tribune's* circulation had reached 11,000. As his daily newspaper grew, Greeley also—like Bennett—published a weekly edition. Circulation of the *Tribune's* weekly edition, aided by cheap mailing rates, eventually rose to 200,000, selling for $2 a year and making Greeley a famous man in the American West.

Bennett's *Herald* took pride in its political independence. As the tensions leading to the Civil War grew, Bennett showed himself to be in favor of slavery. Greeley's paper, on the other hand, initially published a paper aligning itself with the reformist Whig party, and was thoroughly against slavery. As Greeley wrote in his autobiography, "'My leading idea was the establishment of a journal removed alike from servile partisanship on the one hand and mincing neutrality on the other.'"

Greeley sought a middle course, where a journalist could advocate the views of the political party which most appealed to him, and yet "'frankly dissent from its course on a particular question, and even denounce its candidates if they were shown to be deficient in capacity or (far worse) in integrity.'"

Greeley, like Bennett, had substantial newspaper experience before gambling everything to start the *New York Tribune*. His editorial assistant was Henry J. Raymond, newly graduated from the University of Vermont, who earned $8 a week at the *Tribune*. Ten years later Raymond co-founded and was the first editor of the *New York Times*. The *Tribune* rapidly overcame its shaky financial launch, reaching a claimed circulation of 11,000 within seven weeks.

The *Tribune's* pages were about four times the size of the penny papers, and the *Tribune* claimed it gave its readers more reading matter for one cent than any paper ever published. Within four months, Greeley brought in business-savvy manager, Thomas McElrath, to handle the *Tribune's* advertising department. The *Tribune's* rapid success led to vicious competition from *The Sun* and the *Herald*, including beating up the Tribune's newsboys. Greeley in return, attacked his rivals for their news, editorial, and advertising policies.

Perhaps to the surprise of both Bennett and Greeley, the expanding market of news-hungry New York readers made room for the *Tribune*. In fact, by the late 1850s, both the *Herald* and the *Tribune* were really national newspapers, with large New York City circulations multiplied by both newspapers' mailed-out weekly editions. Also, both papers were frequently quoted and discussed by other papers north and south, sometimes with agreement, but often with loathing.

Bennett and Greeley were both editorial geniuses and truly peculiar human beings. With manic energy they overcame poverty to create the two leading newspapers in the United States in the mid-19th Century. By 1850, the *Herald's* daily circulation was claimed to be 100,000, with additional circulation from a weekly edition. The *Tribune* had a daily circulation of 45,000 in the early 1850s but the *Weekly Tribune* circulated 200,000 copies as a virtually national edition by 1860.

EXPANDING NEWS COVERAGE

Bennett's *Herald*, in operation six years before Greeley's *Tribune*, rapidly broadened traditional news coverage in search of more readers.

Bennett followed the lead of Benjamin Day's *Sun*, attracting readers with often-sordid reports from the police stations and the courts. Bennett's paper also covered business and Wall Street news, published reports on high society soirees and theatrical and operatic performances, and outraged some religious leaders with the *Herald's* lengthy reports on annual meetings of religious societies. Sporting events including horse races also found a place in the *Herald's* pages.

After a trip to Europe in 1838, Bennett arranged for correspondents to report to the *Herald* from leading European capitals. In that same year, Bennett attempted to establish Washington correspondents to report on Congress, at the then-substantial sum of $200 per week. For a time, however, that plan was thwarted because the Senate would not allow *Herald* reporters to sit at the higher chambers. Bennett was understandably outraged, seeing this as a ploy to allow Washington newspapers to continue their monopoly on newsgathering there.

Organizationally, the *Herald* succeeded in large because Bennett had hired an able lieutenant, Managing Editor Frederic Hudson, who later wrote one of the early histories of American journalism.

Bennett and his *Herald* were well started on broadening news and newsgathering into recognizably modern forms when Greeley started his *Tribune* in April, 1841. But Greeley's wide-ranging if eccentric mind also launched many innovations. Also, Greeley was much more overtly political than Bennett. Greeley's paper started out backing Whigs, but later turned to the Republican party. Greeley was a political animal, eventually running for president against Ulysses S. Grant in 1873 after being nominated by the Liberal Republicans and the Democrats. He managed to carry six states.

As an editor, Greeley wanted equality for women and men, both in terms of civil rights and in wages paid. He advocated the end of slavery and of imprisonment for debt, and was pro-Temperance—against liquor.

Greeley, with his nearsighted eyes staring through spectacles perched on a moon face garnished with a ruff of whiskers growing on his neck under his chin, spoke in a high-pitched, squeaky voice. He dressed carelessly, resembling a walking unmade bed. He was easy to caricature, but he was arguably the most influential newspaper editor of the 19th Century.

His newspaper staunchly opposed slavery. He embraced spiritualism, crackpot religions, and dabbled in Socialism. Yet he favored greater rights for women, including equal pay for work and voting rights. He saw his newspaper as a forum for a wide range of ideas. True, some prominent journalists labeled Greeley a fraud. On the other hand, editor Joseph Bishop of influential New York Evening Post concluded that Greeley's *Tribune* ". . . was a tremendous force in the country because of the personal faith of the plain people in the honesty of its editor."

5. Convergence, 19th Century style

A technological convergence in the 1840s spurred a communication revolution, a change more seismic for its time than our 21st century convergence. A growing population's demand for more and better news was answered with faster printing presses, a network of railroads that could move newspapers from city to city. The telegraph enabled news to be sent faster than it could be carried for the first time in human history, which led to the development of "wire services" such as the New York Associated Press.

Ever since the War of 1812, Americans wanted more and more news in a greater and greater hurry. Steam power helped, with the development of a network of American railroads, as did steam engines in boats and ships.

The real change, however, arrived in the mid-1840s with the telegraph. Morse-coded messages made possible nearly instantaneous transmission of messages. For the first time in human history, time and space were conquered by what Tom Standage has called "the Victorian Internet," information moving by dots and dashes. Dot—Dot—Dash. That's Morse code for V, as in the long dreamed of victory of instantaneously sending and receiving of messages over great distances.

The telegraph was limited by transmitting over wires strung on poles and by the time and effort needed to send and receive messages. But for its time, it was a more astonishing innovation than the development of the Internet in the 20th century. Public excitement over the telegraph was multiplied in 1858 by the successful laying of a 2,050-mile Atlantic Cable connecting the United States and Europe. The New York jeweler, Tiffany's, took four-inch lengths of left-over cable and sold them as souvenirs.

POPULATION GROWTH AND URBANIZATION

In 1840, the population of the United States was just over 17 million. By 1860, thanks in measure to immigrants flooding into the country, the population had increased to nearly 31.5 million. Over that same two-decade span, the number of newspapers increased by 265 per cent to 3,725, with 387 dailies. There was a democratizing effect caused as an increasing number of working-class Americans read newspapers.

THE RACE FOR NEWS

One innovator was Moses Beach, the brother-in-law to whom Benjamin Day sold his penny paper, the New York Sun. In the 1830s, Beach did his bit to add speed to newsgathering, knowing that readers wanted the newest news. Beach hired William F. Harnden's express service to bring news from the harbors, using a combination of boats and railroad transportation. Using express services, New York newspapers could get their hands on English newspapers arriving at Boston harbor within a day. Beach bragged about his entrepreneurship:

"In consequence of our news-boat arrangements, we receive our papers more than an hour sooner than any other paper in this city. On the arrival of the [ship] *Liverpool* [July 1, 1839], we proceeded to issue an extra, which will reach Albany with the news twelve hours before it will be published in the regular editions of their evening papers, and twenty-four hours ahead of the morning papers."

STEAM POWER AND FASTER PRESSES

The fresher the news, the greater its profitability for newspapers, and profit—greater profit—was the goal.

Increased revenues were reliant on more efficient production of newspapers. As demand for Benjamin Day's *Sun* and James Gordon Bennett's *Herald* grew, faster printing presses were a necessity. For example, *The Sun's* little hand-run rotary press could turn out only 250 sheets an hour, and then Day and a compositor would have to reprint on the other side of the paper.

The Sun increased its paper size to 14 x 20 inches early in 1836 in order to serve more advertisers. As demand for that newspaper rose to about 20,000, *The Sun* began using a Napier press that could print roughly 2,000 copies an hour. By the late 1830s, steam-driven Napier presses could crank out up to 3,000 newspapers in an hour.

A GROWING NETWORK OF RAILROADS

From the beginning of human history until the 1840s, information of any kind could travel no faster than a person could walk or run or a horse could gallop. Moving information over great distances was an age-old challenge.

Stagecoach lines were important in carrying newspapers until largely supplanted by the emergence and rapid growth of railroad networks in the1840s and thereafter. By 1850, there were roughly 6,000 miles of railroad track, mostly in the northern U.S. The Philadelphia Inquirer complained that New York's biggest newspapers were carried "over every railway, sets it [sic] down at every station, and extends it everywhere." Railroads of the 1820s and 1830s could move at the breakneck speed of up to 25 miles an hour.

Railroads added speed and volume to existing mail routes. The one per cent of the mails carried by railroads in 1830 grew to 16 percent by 1837. And by 1843, newspapers made up three quarters of the daily mail sent out of New York City.

For even longer distances, sailing ships carried information across the Atlantic in the form of letters and newspapers from the great cities of Europe. And in the United States, competitive zeal led to the use of homing pigeons with tiny messages in little tubes attached to the bird's legs. Pictures of leading New York newspapers of the early 1840s showed dovecotes on their roofs to accommodate a non-governmental form of "air mail."

REAL MODERNITY BEGINS: THE TELEGRAPH

Americans remember historic dates: July 4, 1776 (publication of the Declaration of Indpendence), December 7, 1941 (Pearl Harbor Day).

But consider this symbolic moment: On May 24, 1844, Samuel F. B. Morse sent a message over wires from the old Supreme Court chamber in Washington, DC to an assistant in Baltimore, MD: "What hath God wrought?" It was this first time ever that humans has been able to communicate instantly over a long distance.

Growth of the telegraph was explosive, as Morse's licensees or competitors using other telegraph patents rapidly strung wire, putting up poles about 20 feet high and 100 yards apart. The experimental telegraph line from Baltimore to Washington, D.C. soon connected to lines to New York and Philadelphia. Other telegraphic trunk lines followed by 1851, linking New York to Boston, another from New York to Buffalo, NY to the Great Lakes, and another from New York to New Orleans.

Remember, before the telegraph, transportation was communication. The telegraph and its possibilities led *Herald* publisher James Gordon Bennett to forecast changes in the newspaper industry. He believed the telegraph would elevate New York City as a communication center and also diminish the power of politics and political money over the Washington press. Bennett wrote:

"By means of the telegraph the local advantages of the Washington papers are transferred to this metropolis, and the superior enterprise and pecuniary means of the journals here will enable them to turn these advantages to the best account. Next session of Congress. . . [w]e will give telegraphic reports of congressional debates and proceedings which will defy competition and fully satisfy the whole country. As for official or semi-official information to be obtained in Washington, will be able to give it here, and diffuse it throughout the country, before the indolent papers in that remote village [Washington, D.C.] have printed it in their columns.

"As matters stand there, no newspaper can exist in Washington without receiving the wages of corruption from Congress, in the shape of jobs and gratuities."

Bennett's prediction about making New York the center of news in America was accurate, but not for the *Herald*-centric treasons he offered. The key was the New York Associated Press, a cooperative owned by New York City's most powerful newspapers: the *Courier and Enquirer*, the *Express*, the *Herald*, the *Journal of Commerce*, *The Sun*, the *Times*, and the *Tribune*. As historian Maury Klein has depicted the AP, it was the result of convergence among New York's top newspapers with the telegraph and wire service news. "News via the telegraph," Klein declared, "made the nation more dependent on New York for news because the Associated Press dominated telegraph dispatches and the New York City Press controlled the Associated Press."

Bennett's *Herald* made especially heavy use of the telegraph as it then existed in reporting the far-off U.S.–Mexican War of 1846-1848. When the Mexican War began, there were no telegraph lines to the West across the nation, and telegraph lines reached only as far South as Richmond, VA. As historian Edwin Emery wrote, New Orleans daily newspapers were closest to the battles in Mexico and their war coverage gave them prominence. Bennett invested in newsgathering, starting a pony express the nation, but soon shared that effort with the *Baltimore Sun*.

CONVERGING WITH TODAY

James Gordon Bennett and Horace Greeley were only part of the story as daily newspapers evolved into recognizably modern forms. Their long careers, however, may be taken as symbols of a new age in communication. Their working lives spanned a time when newspapers were really cottage industries, sheets produced on clunky hand-cranked presses and filled with items reprinted from other items newspapers or that were dropped off in the printing house.

They started their newspapers—Bennett in 1835 and Greeley in 1841—as penny papers with virtually no capital investment and aimed at an upwardly mobile society which wanted newspapers for the common person, not for the elite. Their success saw greater and greater demand, the need for faster and faster printing, and for organized newsgathering using a new form of employee—the reporter.

These papers saw the transformation over about 25 years of newspapers into industries. Large daily newspapers became major industrial plants requiring substantial capital investment, as well as many employees in buildings housing expensive and elaborate steam-driven printing presses.

Early in the 21st century, media convergence has become a common (if over-used) term. Generally, it is taken to mean using digital technology to combine multiple media platforms, or merging print, television, and radio with interactive, Web-capable technologies.

The Internet was built in a time of satellite transmission of messages, so immediacy in sending and receiving information world-wide was nothing new by the Millennium of 2000.

But what is past is prologue: the roots of modern communication and the media of 21st century are firmly planted in mid-19th century newspaper wars, and in the inventions and innovations aggressive editors so enthusiastically put to use to gather news and to conquer space and time.

The First Amendment

The First Amendment to the U.S. Constitution protects five important freedoms: religion, speech, press, assembly and petition. Even though the First Amendment has been in the Constitution for almost the entire history of the republic, the idea of its protective powers has been slow to develop.

This chapter on the First Amendment is a standard part of almost all of the titles in the Tennessee Journalism Series.

Religion

Many Americans have their history wrong. They believe that the first European settlers of this nation came to America because they believed in the right to practice religion and worship freely.

Actually, many of them came because they wanted to practice their religion freely. They did not care about the right of people outside their own groups to observe a different set of beliefs.

During the colonial years there was a much religious intolerance and state supported religion practice as there was in England or any place else in Europe.

But that began to change in the late 18th century, particularly through the writing and efforts of Thomas Jefferson, who challenged the government's role in religious observance.

Freedom of religion today

Today, through many events and court cases, we have developed some fundamental understandings about what the words of the First Amendment mean (sometimes referred to as the 'establishment clause'):

Individuals have the right to believe, practice religion, and worship as they see fit.

Individuals are not required to support any religion or religious organization.

The government cannot establish or support any religious organization.

The government must remain neutral in dealing with religious organizations and beliefs.

Even with these fundamental understandings, there are still many controversies and issues surrounding the First Amendment's guarantee of freedom of religion and of the state neutrality toward religion. For instance, consider these:

> – prayer in schools

> – creationism

> – posting the Ten Commandments in government buildings

> – requiring the recitation of the Pledge of Allegiance in schools

– blue laws

– putting Christmas decorations on public property

The list could go on.

Speech

If the First Amendment means anything, we believe, it means that we have the right to speak our minds — to say what we think, right?

That's correct.

But it wasn't always so.

In the early days of the republic, laws were passed that protected the president and administration from criticism.

Many states had laws restricting the freedom of speech, especially in the South where is was against the law to advocate abolition (freeing slaves). Yet Americans have always enjoyed debating the issues of the day. They like to argue, disagree, and even diss one another. From colonial days Americans have sought solutions to social, economic and political problems by vigorous and animated discussion. Sometimes those discussions have turned violent. More often than not, however, the discussions have ultimately resulted in commonly agreed upon solutions and principles.

Despite its halting beginning, "free speech" proved its value more than once, and the concept is now deeply embedded in the American psyche.

Still, as much as we honor free speech, we are sometimes not very careful in preserving it. Our tendency to censor speech that is disturbing or disagreeable -- or that doesn't agree with what seems to be the majority opinion -- sometimes gets the best of us. We also have a tendency to think that if we limit speech in certain ways and on certain topics, we can solve some pressing social problem. Particularly during national crises, we tend to believe that if we can just stop people from saying certain things, our nation will be more secure.

When we do this, however, we are defying our own best instincts and a logic that experience teaches again and again. We can never successfully keep people from saying what they believe in, from believing whatever they choose, and from expressing those beliefs publicly. Other societies try doing this, and eventually they explode.

People do not like to be told that they cannot say something.

Neither do we.

Our job as Americans is to protect free speech wherever it is threatened. We should constantly be on guard against the thinking that restricting speech will somehow make us a better society. We should preserve our unique place in the world as a society who values its individual citizens and protects them even when they say or do things that are not popular.

Press

This part of the First Amendment

'. . . or of the press . . .'

has generated a great deal of debate and much litigation throughout the history of the republic.

Just what did the founders of the Republic mean by that? How have we interpreted that phrase since it was originally written?

Answers to those questions have filled many volumes, but generally we believe that the government should not censor printed material; that it should not exercise prior restraint (preventing something from being printed or distributed) on publications; and that it should not hinder the distribution of printed material.

In journalism, this freedom extends to the practice of journalism itself. Reporters should be able to gather information. Government bodies – courts, legislative units, boards, etc. – should operate in the open. Government records should be available to all citizens who request them. In some cases, reporters are protected from disclosing their sources because of this clause in the First Amendment.

Two important areas where the freedom to publish is limited are: libel or defamation; and copyright and trademark.

Libel or defamation

Libel – the concept that words can harm a person's reputation – is an ancient principle of common law. A person's reputation has value, and when that value is diminished, a person can see redress from the courts.

Yet there is the First Amendment, which says society has value in being able to speak freely. How do we resolve this conflict?

Despite the language of the First Amendment, libel laws exist and are, occasionally, enforced. Journalists must be careful about libel.

Modern defamation laws say that to win a libel case, you must prove

- publication (more than just two people have to see/hear it)

- identification (can the person defamed be identified)
- defamation (did the words have potential to do real damage)
- fault (was there negligence or some mitigation)
- harm (is there provable damage)

Defenses against defamation

Statute and case law provide some strong defenses for people facing libel actions:

• truth – powerful defense (society values truth)

• qualified privilege – is the situation one that relieves people of libel responsibility? Reporters depend on the concept of qualified privilege to report public affairs. For instance, they may report the arrest of a person who is ultimately is declared innocent of a crime.

• absolute privilege – Some instances, such as a legislator speaking in a meeting of the legislature, can say anything he or she wishes without regard to libel laws.

• statute of limitations – Courts do not like old cases, particularly in civil matters. Many states have a statue of limitations provision that says a libel suit must be filed within two years of the alleged libel.

• Constitutional privilege – This privilege protects news media from suits by public officials and public figures. It comes from a 1964 decision, New York Times v Sullivan. The results of this case make virtually impossible for any well known figure to recover damages in a libel action.

Still, the threat of the costs of litigation are real, and journalists should be careful to avoid them if possible.

Copyright

The freedom to write and publish is not unlimited.

One area in which that freedom is limited is that of copyright and trademarks, which are part of a larger area of law known as intellectual property. People who create what we might term generally as "intellectual property" – books, musical works, art, sculpture, articles, poems, etc. – have some protection in the way that those works are used by others. If you draw a picture or write a poem, that picture or poem is yours (at least for a limited amount of time), and no one else can reprint it without your permission.

There are things that copyright does not cover, however.

Facts cannot be copyrighted. Let's say you are the only writer covering your high school basketball game, and you write a story about it for the high school paper. Another publication can take the facts that you have described – the details of the game, the score, etc. – and use them in its description of the game.

That publication, however, cannot use your account of the game. The expression of facts can be copyrighted, but the facts themselves cannot.

Like facts, ideas cannot be copyrighted, but the expression of those ideas can. For instance, you can paint a picture of a tree, and that painting will be copyrighted. Someone else can paint a picture of the same tree. That's ok, as long as they do not use your painting.

The protection of a copyright is limited in two important ways. One is that it does not last forever. Currently, copyrights last for the life of the creator, plus 70 years. If the copyright is owned by a corporation, the copyright lasts longer. A copyright does not last forever. At some point, all creative works become part of the "public domain"; that is, everyone owns them. Consequently, the works of William Shakespeare, for instance, are in the public domain, and Shakespeare can be quoted at length without anyone's permission.

The second limitation of copyright is through the concept of fair use. This concept has been developed to encourage the dissemination of ideas and information without either putting a great burden on the user or infringing on the rights of the creator of the work. Fair use means that in certain limited circumstances, a copyrighted work – or more likely, some portion of it – may be used without the permission of the holder of the copyright.

Courts have looked at four things in considering what is fair use:

– the nature of the copyrighted material – how much effort it took to produce it;

– the nature of the use – for instance, material used in an educational setting for educational purposes is more likely to be thought of as fair use;

– the extent of the use – how much of the copyrighted material is used, just a few words or a whole passage;

– commercial infringement – most importantly, how much does the use hurt the commercial value of the work.

Unless material is being used in a very limited way, you should always get permission to use copyrighted material. Holders of copyright can be very aggressive about enforcing their copyrights, and the unauthorized user of a copyright can be fined substantially. Many people in education believe that they can use any material in any way they wish, and it will be considered fair use. That is not the case. Educators are bound by copyright laws as much as anyone else.

Note: Material on the Internet has as much copyright protection as anything else. Some people believe that whatever is on a web site is in the public domain, and that is not the case. Just because material is easy to access does not mean that it does not have copyright protection.

Trademark

A special protection for the commercial use of words, phrases and symbols is trademark.

Many companies go to great lengths to protect their trademarks because that is how the public identifies their products. What if, for example, a shoe company named Nuke started using the Nike symbol, the swoosh, on its shoes? Consumers might become confused about what product to buy, and Nike, which holds a trademark on the swoosh, might be hurt by that.

Assembly

The First Amendment guarantees that people can get together –
peaceably – and talk about whatever they want to discuss.

Courts have almost always recognized that governments have the power
to regulate time and place of assembly when the public's safety and
convenience is an issue.

But governments are prevented from saying to a group of people that
they cannot meet when the reason for their meeting is legal.

According to the First Amendment Center:

First Amendment freedoms ring hollow if government officials can
repress expression that they fear will create a disturbance or offend.
Unless there is real danger of imminent harm, assembly rights must be
respected.

About the picture:

*Before 1920, most women in the United States could not vote. In the 19th
century, they had few legal rights at all, and the social customs against women
being seen in public unless they were with another woman or accompanied by a
man were strict and unacceptable by today's standards. When women starting
petitioning for the right to vote in the early part of the 20th century, they began
holding parades, exercising their right to assembly. Here is the beginning of the
Washington Suffrage Parade of 1913, a significant event in the history of the
suffrage movement. For more information on this parade and its effect on the
eventual passage of the Nineteenth Amendment, go to Seeing Suffrage.*

Petition

When an individual

• calls the tax assessor's office to complain that property taxes have gone up too much,

• attends a town meeting public officials and policies are questioned,

• joins a legal street demonstration to gain publicity for their cause,

• pays a lobbyist or joins a group that pays someone to go to Washington or the state capital to argue for a cause,

then that person is petitioning 'the Government for a redress of grievances' – a right protected by the First Amendment.

The right to petition the government was very much on the minds of the Founding Fathers. As colonists, they had asked King George III and the government in London many times to pay attention to what they wanted. Mostly, the people in England ignored them.

So, when it came time to write the Declaration of Independence, they included the following in their reasons for declaring independence:

In every state of these Oppressions We have Petitioned for Redress in the most humble terms: Our repeated Petitions have been answered only by repeated injury.

Governments in the U.S. do not have to agree with the petitioner or do what he or she asks. But they must listen.

And they cannot retaliate against the petitioner for asking.

Compared to the other parts of the First Amendment, the right to petition the government has not generated much litigation or attention among scholars over the years. Perhaps, according to Adam Newton, writing for the First Amendment Center, that is because it continues to work so well. The petition clause is the tacit assumption in constitutional analysis, the primordial right from which other expressive freedoms arise. Why speak, why publish, why assemble against the government at all if such complaints will only be silenced?

About the picture:

Mary Gertrude Fendall (left) and Mary Dubrow (right) standing outside what is likely National Woman's Party headquarters, holding between them a large sign containing text of a Resolution Addressed to Senator Edward J. Gay with a long unrolled sheet of paper, presumably signatures on a petition, laying on the ground in front of them. The sign was in support of the Nineteenth Amendment, which would given women the right to vote. The sign mentions mentions that "President Woodrow Wilson has urged the passage of the Federal Suffrage amendment before the Senate of the United States and again recently before the whole Congress of the United States as a necessary War and Reconstruction Measure . . ." Wilson first publicly declared his support for the amendment on Jan. 9, 1918. He asked the Senate to pass the amendment as a war measure on Sept. 30, 1918. The amendment was passed in the House on May 21, 1919, and in the Senate on June 4, 1919. Library of Congress photos, circa 1918-1919.

History

First Amendment Videos

Gitlow v. New York

Videos of Dr. Dwight Teeter discussing various aspects of the First Amendment and how it developed can be found at these links:

https://vimeo.com/9852487

https://vimeo.com/9754284

https://vimeo.com/9748541

https://vimeo.com/9823451

https://vimeo.com/9772215

The First Amendment grew our of four concepts of behavior of human beings in society (as identified by Teeter, Le Duc, and Loving):

• marketplace of ideas

• individual fulfillment

• safety valve

• self-governance

Each of the concepts is important for an understanding of why people in the 18th century -- the time when America earned its independence from Great Britain and adopted the Constitution -- believed in the notion of freedom of speech.

The marketplace of ideas is based on the concept that no one person or entity knows the truth that can be applied to every action of mankind. Since no human has the authority to say what is right or wrong or true or not true, ideas must be expressed and tested. The famous English author John Milton gave voice to the marketplace of ideas (although he did not use that term), and many in the 18th century followed his line of thinking. Simply put, the concept is that if everyone can express his or her ideas, the truth will eventually emerge.

Individual fulfillment means that all people have potential to become more than they area. As humans, they need the freedom to express themselves and to try to expand and improve their character and productivity. By doing this, they are of benefit to the entire society. People can define themselves through their individual expressions.

The idea of freedom of speech as a safety valve means that individuals can express opposition to authority without punishment, and this -- in the long run -- has a calming effect on the political society. If people know that at the very least they can speak and be heard, they are less likely to rebel against the whole structure of the state.

Finally, free speech is the basis of self governance. No society can claim to have its people self governing if it does not allow free expression of ideas.

These ideas were floating around and much debate when America won its independence from Great Britain in the 1780s. A great deal of free speech had already been practiced by the Founding Fathers as they were making war against Britain and as they were setting up their own government, so individual rights did not seem like a critical issue.

But as Americans debated the ratification of a new Constitution in 1787 and 1788, many prominent people -- people such as Patrick Henry and Samuel Adams -- opposed the Constitution because they believed that it would concentrate too much power in the hands of two few people. Individual liberties -- the right to speak and to assemble, for instance -- would be threatened by the newly powerful centralized authorities.

To counter those arguments, proponents of the Constitution promised that, once the document was ratified and put into place, they would support a set of amendments that would guarantee the rights about which the opponents were concerned. James Madison, who had been a chief architect of the Constitution itself, took the lead in drafting these amendments, which eventually became known as the Bill of Rights.

The First Amendment is the first of 10 of these amendments. Some deal with individual liberties. Others deal with how the government much handle individuals accused of a crime. Still others restrict government action in certain areas.

The First Amendment is not first because the Founding Fathers considered it the most important one. The historical record indicates that they clearly did not. Still, the fact that it is first has invested it with much value. What is means exactly is still a matter of vigorous debate.

The politics of the First Amendment

The First Amendment, as Professor Teeter says in the video in the previous section, is "the chance product of political expediency." (He's quoting Leonard Levy, another First Amendment scholar.) How did that happen?

James Madison was the chief author of the new Constitution that had been put forth by those wanting to form a strong central government in 1787. As such, Madison became one of the leaders in arguing for its ratification. The Constitution was the product of weeks of delicate compromise on many of its points, and Madison feared that any changes to it would destroy its chance for passage.

That's exactly what the opponents of the Constitution hoped, and they began complaining that the Constitution did not protect individuals from the powers of government to take away civil liberties, such as freedom of speech, freedom of the press and the right to trial by jury. This debate took place in just about every state that considered the Constitution but it was conducted fiercely in Virginia, Madison's home state. Opponents were led by Patrick Henry, the popular orator of the Revolution and a man still active in politics. Henry and other feared a powerful central government.

Sitting on the fence in this debate were the Virginia Baptists and other religious groups who had been fighting against the established and official religion of the Anglican church. Baptists were persuaded by these argument -- especially by the lack of separation of church and state.

This put them and James Madison in an awkward position. Madison and the Baptists had been strong allies in the fight against an established church. Now, Madison appeared to be abandoning that principle with his support for this new Constitution.

In truth, Madison did not think that these rights needed to be protected by the new Constitution, and he feared that adding them would upset the fine balance he had struck to complete the Constitution to begin with. But recognized and understood the concerns of his friends, the Baptists. He also knew that without their support, it would be unlikely that Virginia would ratify the Constitution. And if Virginia, the largest state among the original 13 colonies, did not do so, the Constitution itself would not be ratified.

So, Madison promised to support a bill of rights that would be added to the Constitution after it had been ratified and the first government had been established. He promised to run for Congress and then to do what he could to introduce the necessary amendments. That stance put Madison in the position of admitting that there was something lacking about the Constitution that he so ardently supported. Still, he did want was necessary and was able to persuade the Baptists and other concerned religious groups to his side.

The Constitution was ultimately ratified, and the new government was put in place.

Madison was elected to the Congress but initially found little support among his colleagues for immediately amending the Constitution before it had had a chance to work. Still, he had made a promise, and he used his massive intellect and political skill to keep that promise

As historian Forrest Church has written:

His (Madison's) authorship of the First Amendment constitutes perhaps his most abiding legacy. Acting on the crucial impetus provided by his Baptist constituents, he etched church-state separate and freedom of conscience into the American code.

For more on the ratification battles over the U.S. Constitution, see the Teaching American History website.

The First Amendment in the 19th
and early 20th centuries

By the early 1790s, the First Amendment, along with the other nine amendments that constituted the Bill of Rights, had been ratified -- and seemingly quickly forgotten. During the single term of the John Adams presidency (1797 - 1800), Congress passed and the president signed the Alien and Sedition Acts that outlawed criticism of the president and those in power. (Figure -.-)

Republicans such as Thomas Jefferson and James Madison -- in opposition to the Federalists -- could do little about these acts. The Supreme Court had not yet established itself as the body that could review laws passed by Congress for their constitutionality, so there was at that point no check on congressional power. The acts themselves were ineffective in stifling criticism of the president, and fortunately, they expired after two years. By that time, Thomas Jefferson had been elected president, and the Federalists would never return to power. The Alien and Sedition Acts stained the Adams presidency, and they made heroes out of those they meant to persecute.

The First Amendment and the other parts of the Bill of Rights were meant to restrain Congress. People of the early republic saw their power and intent as limited. States and state constitutions were still the source of governmental power that Americans recognized as most important. Recall that the First Amendment begins with the words: "Congress shall make no law . . ." This phrase was deliberate and taken seriously by the people of the time. Congress could not make laws, but states certainly could.

In addition, we need to understand that the greatest concern of those who composed the First Amendment was religious liberty and the free exercise of religious practices -- not free expression. Madison, Jefferson and their allies wanted to prevent the new government from establishing an official church -- not guaranteeing free speech or a free press. They wanted to build a "wall of separation" between the government and the church.

In this, they were highly successful. Religious liberty and the free exercise of religion -- without interference from the government became an established principle of the nation. It is one that remains in effect today, so much so that we often take it for granted.

But the idea of freedom of expression had a tougher time.

The chief and abiding political and moral issue facing American in the first half of the 19th century was slavery. Slave had been in America for 300 years by that time, and slavery had worked its way into the social, political and economic system. As tobacco and cotton -- particularly cotton -- grew in importance, slavery as a means of producing these products also strengthened.

The emotional and political costs were enormous.

Whites, especially those in the South where slavery existed and grew, lived in constant fear that slaves would one day rise up in bloody revolt. Those fears were not groundless. Slaves in the newly formed nation of Haiti had done just that, and every Southern plantation resident had nightmares that the same thing would happen on their land, even though they might fool themselves into thinking that their slaves were happy and contented.

Northerners shared many of those fears, and because their economic systems did not depend so much of cotton and tobacco, Northern states were able to free themselves slowly from the slavery system. Still, the fear of the possibility of a slave revolt was national.

Consequently, those who advocated freedom for slaves -- emancipationists and abolitionists -- were not welcome in many places. Southern states passed laws against the printing and distribution of abolitionist newspapers. They also outlawed the open advocacy of emancipation or abolition. In some cases, newspaper editors who wrote about such things had their presses destroyed, were run out of town, or in a few tragic instances killed. Clearly, these situations offend our 21st century ideas of what the First Amendment should mean, but most people of the time did not view the First Amendment in this fashion.

One man who did was a Kentucky newspaper editor named Cassius Marcellus Clay. Clay had come from a slave-holding family in Kentucky but during his college days at Yale had been persuaded that slavery was wrong. He became an emancipationist, someone who advocated the gradual freeing of slaves. (Abolitionists favored immediate freedom for slaves.) Clay was stubborn and tough. He was criticized harshly for his stance and physically attacked several times for what he wrote about slavery.

Clay was one of the few men of the 19th century to say that the First Amendment to the Constitution should protect people like him from any government intrusion.

The nation did not hear or heed Clay, and those who advocated unpopular ideas were subjected to legal and extra-legal pressures to conform or remain silent. During the Civil War, Lincoln and his administration brought government power to bear against those they felt were endangering the war efforts.

The one bright spot in the 19th century for civil liberties came in 1868 when the nation ratified the 14th Amendment, which said that states could not deprive people of liberty or proper without resorting to "due process of law" and could not deny people the "equal protection" of the law. This amendment was put in place to assure that freed slaves would be given their full rights in states where slavery has previously be prevalent. This was clearly a check on state power and an assertion that the U.S. Constitution was the ultimate law of the land. It was another 50 years before this idea -- that states had to be subject to the will of the federal constitution -- took hold in any meaningful sense. When it did, in a 1925 Supreme Court ruling, it changed the entire balance of legal power in the United States and set us on the road to our modern thinking about First Amendment protections.

Meanwhile, America endured several national crises, including what was then known as the Great War (1914 - 1918). We call it World War I today. It was a time, more than any other in the nation's history, when the American government, under the direction of Woodrow Wilson, strayed from the principle of protecting free expression.

In 1917, the year America entered the war, Congress passed the Espionage Act which made it a crime "to willfully cause or attempt to cause insubordination, disloyalty, mutiny, or refusal of duty, in the military or naval forces of the United States," or to "willfully obstruct the recruiting or enlistment service of the United States."

The next year saw passage of the Sedition Act, which outlawed spoken or printed criticism of the U.S. government, the Constitution or the flag.

The Wilson administration was vigorous in using these laws and other means to suppress dissent. Part of the woman suffrage movement -- the Woman Political Party led by Alice Paul -- were particularly irritating to the administration. Despite America's entry into the war, members of the NWP continued to picket the White House, demanding that Wilson support suffrage at home while he was touting the expansion of democracy abroad.

The women picketers were arrested for "obstructing sidewalk traffic" and hauled off to jail. At first, their sentences were relatively light (two to six days in many cases), and the administration hoped the arrests would discourage future demonstrations. The opposite occurred.

Women continued to picket the White House, and the signs they carried grew more pointed. When they were rearrested, they were given longer sentences. The women asked to be treated as political prisoners, a status they were denied. They then we on hunger strikes. Prison officials, with the administration's approval, subjected the women the women to forced feeding, a torture process that kept the women alive but weakened and injured them.

Once out of jail, the suffragists continued to picket the White House and tell the story of what happened to them at the hands of government officials -- all for non-violently demanding their political rights. The picketing and protests continued after the war and up until the passage of the 19th Amendment that gave women the right to vote.

The treatment the suffragists received was not as harsh that meted out to those charged and convicted under the Espionage and Sedition Acts. Some people spend years in prison for the crime of protesting the nation's involvement in the Great War -- violating the rights to speech and petition that the First Amendment was supposed to protect.

Courts were of little use in protecting these rights. The Supreme Court on numerous occasions had the opportunity to check the administration's actions but failed to do so.

As America came out of the war, many people were disturbed by the heavy-handedness of the Wilson administration in suppressing dissent. They believed that America was in danger of losing its way as the beacon of free societies and that more attention should be paid to actively protecting civil liberties than to simply saying that "Congress shall make no law . . ."

This change in attitude did not occur all at once. Rather, it was a step-by-step process that began with the Supreme Court ruling in Gitlow v. New York in 1925. In that decision, for the first time, the Court said that because of the 14th Amendment, Constitutional protections, such as those in the First Amendment, applied to state actions. This decision opened the door for a wide variety of other decisions during the next 40 years that strengthened protections guaranteed by the Bill of Rights.

11773524R00026

Printed in Great Britain
by Amazon